Evening Meals
Around the World

by **Michele Zurakowski**

illustrated by **Jeff Yesh**

Thanks to our advisers for their
expertise, research, and advice:

JoAnne Buggey, Ph.D., Elementary Social Studies
College of Education and Human Development
University of Minnesota, Minneapolis
Member, National Council for the Social Studies

Susan Kesselring, M.A., Literacy Educator
Rosemount-Apple Valley-Eagan (Minnesota) School District

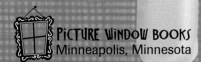

PICTURE WINDOW BOOKS
Minneapolis, Minnesota

The editor wishes to thank Susanne Mattison, Culinary Specialist for Byerly's,
for her expert advice on preparing the recipes for this book.

Managing Editor: Bob Temple
Creative Director: Terri Foley
Editor: Sara E. Hoffmann
Editorial Adviser: Andrea Cascardi
Copy Editor: Laurie Kahn
Designer: Nathan Gassman
Page production: Picture Window Books
The illustrations in this book were rendered digitally.

Picture Window Books
1710 Roe Crest Drive
North Mankato, MN 56003
www.capstonepub.com

*For Aidan and Cian,
with hope for your palates
—M.Z.*

Library of Congress Cataloging-in-Publication Data
Zurakowski, Michele.
Evening meals around the world / by Michele Zurakowski ;
illustrated by Jeff Yesh.
p. cm. – (Meals around the world)
Summary: Discusses the variety of foods people around the world
might have for their evening meals.
ISBN-13: 978-1-4048-0282-7 (library binding)
ISBN-10: 1-4048-0282-7 (library binding)
ISBN-13: 978-1-4048-1132-4 (paperback)
ISBN-10: 1-4048-1132-X (paperback)
1. Dinners and dining—Juvenile literature. 2. Cookery,
International—Juvenile literature.
[1. Dinners and dining. 2. Food habits.] I. Yesh, Jeff, 1971- ill. II. Title.
III. Series.
TX737.Z87 2004
641.5'4—dc22   2003016441

For some people, the evening meal is the biggest of the day. For others, it is small. Some people eat thick soups and crunchy salads. Others munch on warm breads and spicy stews.

Right now, somewhere in the world, families are sitting down to their evening meals.

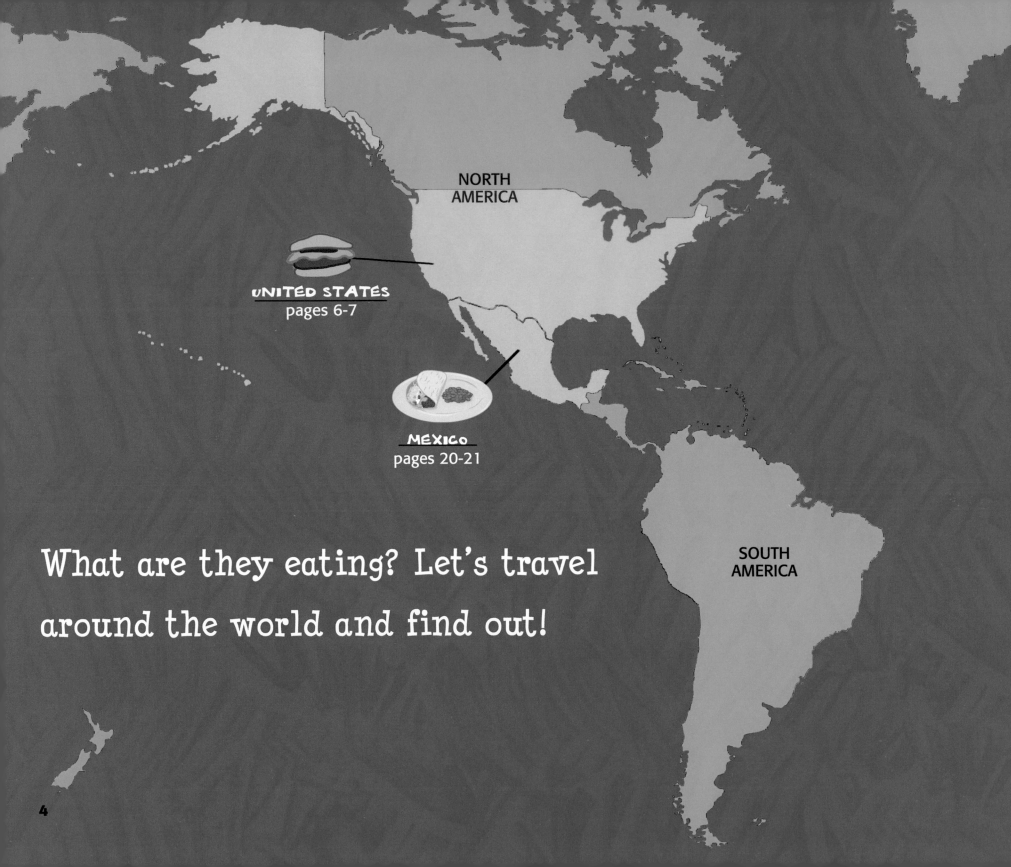

NORTH
AMERICA

UNITED STATES
pages 6-7

MEXICO
pages 20-21

SOUTH
AMERICA

What are they eating? Let's travel around the world and find out!

EUROPE

ASIA

ITALY
pages 18-19

CHINA
page 10

VIETNAM
page 11

MOROCCO
pages 16-17

ETHIOPIA
pages 12-13

INDIA
pages 14-15

AFRICA

AUSTRALIA
pages 8-9

AUSTRALIA

Many American kids like to eat hamburgers.

A hamburger is a patty of beef served on a round bun. But that's only the beginning. Ketchup, mustard, pickles, onions, and lettuce all can be added to turn a hamburger into a great evening meal.

American Evening Meal

- hamburger
- fruit
- vegetables
- chocolate ice cream

7

Lamb is the most popular meat in Australia. Australians chop it, fry it, or eat it served as a grilled, juicy lamb chop.

After their meals, Australian children get out their spoons for a special treat. A pavlova (pav-LOH-vah) is a sweet, creamy meringue overflowing with pieces of fresh fruit.

Australian Evening Meal

• lamb chops
• mashed potatoes
• asparagus
• pavlova
• milk

The evening meal in China is a time for sharing. Families pass around steaming bowls of rice and everyone takes a helping. Children and grown-ups use chopsticks to pick up crunchy stir-fried vegetables or pork with sweet walnuts.

Chinese Evening Meal

- rice
- vegetable stir-fry
- pork with sweet walnuts
- egg-drop soup
- asparagus salad
- watermelon
- jasmine tea

Peanuts make a tasty snack, but in Vietnam peanuts can be part of the evening meal. The nuts are crushed and cooked into a thick sauce. Thin slices of chicken are threaded onto wooden skewers. After the chicken is grilled, families dip it into the sweet peanut sauce before each bite. Yum! Vietnamese children call this dish chicken *satay* (sa-TAY).

Vietnamese Evening Meal

- rice
- grilled chicken *satay* and peanut sauce
- shredded cabbage salad
- mango
- bananas with ice cream

11

In Ethiopia, people often eat a thin bread called *injera* (in-JEE-ra). One large *injera* can feed the whole family.

Everyone breaks off a hunk of the bread. They use the *injera* to scoop up tasty stews and spicy sauces. When the meal is finished, there are no forks or spoons to wash.

Ethiopian Evening Meal

- *injera*
- goat stew
- steamed greens
- fried plantains

13

Kids get to stay up late in India. The evening meal is served at night to make sure everyone is home from work or school and can eat together.

Vegetables and rice are a popular weekday meal. Meat is saved for weekends and holidays. Each day, people eat lentil dal (LEN-tul DOLL), a buttery, soupy dish made from tiny beans. They also might have tea or cool lemonade mixed with rose-water.

Indian Evening Meal

- vegetables
- rice
- spinach curry
- chapatis
- chutney
- lentil dal
- lemonade with rosewater

Grab a cushion when you sit down for an evening meal in Morocco. In this country, everyone sits on the floor and gathers around a low table. The meal gets busy when people start passing the couscous (KOOS-koos).

Small bites of meat are sometimes added to couscous to bring good luck. Some couscous is sprinkled with cinnamon. What a sweet way to eat your evening meal!

Moroccan Evening Meal

- couscous
- pita bread
- dates
- mint tea

17

In Italy, the evening meal lasts a long time. After you eat one tasty dish, another one is served.

Italian Evening Meal

• pizza
• fillet of fish
• salad
• cheese
• fruit
• gelato

Start your meal with a hot, yummy pizza. That's how families eat in Campania, on the west coast of Italy. Next comes a crispy, fried fillet of fish served in tomato sauce. But you're still not finished. Have a fresh green salad. Have a chunk of cheese. Have room for dessert?

The evening meal in Mexico is just one course. Sometimes families don't cook at all! Often, Mexican families stroll down the street and stop at a taqueria (ta-kah-REE-yah) to buy some tacos.

TAQUERIA

If families stay home for their evening meals, they might eat beans and tortillas (tor-TEE-yuhs). Everyone might gather in the kitchen and fix scrambled eggs or sandwiches. The evening meal is a time for families to be together.

Mexican Evening Meal

- tacos or beans and tortillas
- eggs or sandwiches
- sweet roll
- milk

21

All around the world, families enjoy sharing food with each other in the evening. Sometimes they eat big meals with many courses. Sometimes they like simpler meals. But everyone seems to like saying good-bye to the day with food. What are you having for *your* evening meal tonight?

Try These Fun Recipes

You Can Make Couscous

Makes 1 serving

What you need: water, 1 teaspoon (5 ml) olive oil, couscous

What to do:

1. In a medium saucepan, bring 1/2 cup (118 ml) of water and olive oil just to a boil.

2. Stir in the couscous and cover the saucepan.

3. Remove the pan from heat and let the couscous stand in the pan for 5 minutes.

4. Fluff the couscous lightly with a fork, and serve it on a plate or platter.

5. If you want to be like a Moroccan child, you can add bits of vegetables and meat to your couscous.

Make sure you have an adult to help you.

You Can Make
Vietnamese Bananas with Ice Cream

Makes 4 servings

What you need:
2 bananas
2 tablespoons (30 grams) butter or margarine
2 tablespoons (30 grams) firmly packed brown sugar
4 scoops vanilla ice cream
4 teaspoons (20 grams) grated coconut

What to do:

1. Peel the bananas. Cut them into 1-inch (2 1/2-centimeter) slices.

2. Melt the butter or margarine in a large skillet over medium heat.

3. Stir in the brown sugar with a wooden spoon.
   Be sure to get all the lumps out.

4. Add the banana slices to the pan. Cook about 3 minutes until they
   are lightly browned. Turn them over. Cook on the other side
   until they are lightly browned.

5. Scoop the ice cream into four bowls.
   Top with the warm bananas.

6. Sprinkle each bowl with 1 teaspoon (5 grams)
   of grated coconut.

Make sure
you have an
adult to
help you.

Fun Facts

- In West Africa, cooks like to prepare a whole meal in one pot. It uses less fuel to cook, and there is only one pot to wash!

- Spaghetti noodles are made out of wheat. The grains of wheat are ground into flour. Flour, salt, and water are mixed together to make dough. The dough can be cut into all kinds of shapes—fat tubes, curlicues, and bow ties. All the shapes made from this dough are called pasta.

- Jasmine rice is a special kind of rice that grows in Vietnam. When it is cooked, the grains of jasmine rice stick together. This makes it easier to eat with chopsticks.

- In Morocco, you might not eat with a spoon or a fork or chopsticks. Instead, you might eat with your right hand. Using your fingers, you would push your couscous into little balls. Then, you would pop the balls into your mouth. You also might use pita bread as a scoop.

Glossary

chapati—a round flat bread made of whole wheat flour

chutney—a mixture of cooked fruits or vegetables. Chutney can be sweet, sour, or spicy.

curry—a blend of spices that is used to flavor many foods. Curry is also the name for a spicy, stew-like dish.

meringue—a creamy dessert made from egg whites and sugar

plantain—a tropical fruit that looks like a banana but cannot be eaten raw

shredded—cut up into thin strips

skewer—a small wooden stick used for cooking food over a fire

taqueria—a small shop where you can buy tacos and burritos

To Learn More

At the Library
Compestine, Ying Chang. *The Story of Noodles*. New York: Holiday House, 2002.

Cook, Deanna F. *The Kids' Multicultural Cookbook: Food & Fun Around the World*. Charlotte, Vt.: Williamson Pub. Co., 1995.

Friedman, Ina R. *How My Parents Learned to Eat*. Boston: Houghton Mifflin, 1984.

Lauber, Patricia. *What You Never Knew About Fingers, Forks & Chopsticks*. New York: Simon & Schuster Books for Young Readers, 1999.

Schuette, Sarah L. *An Alphabet Salad: Fruits and Vegetables from A to Z*. Mankato, Minn.: A+ Books, 2003.

On the Web
Fact Hound offers a safe, fun way to find Web sites related to this book. All of the sites on Fact Hound have been researched by our staff.

1. Visit *www.facthound.com*
2. Type in this special code: 1404802827
3. Click on the FETCH IT button.

Your trusty Fact Hound will fetch the best sites for you!

Index